Thread Count

Terri Kirby Erickson

1663 Liberty Drive, Suite 200
Bloomington, Indiana 47403
(800) 839-8640
www.AuthorHouse.com

© 2006 Terri Kirby Erickson. All Rights Reserved.

No part of this book may be reproduced, stored in a retrieval system, or transmitted by any means without the written permission of the author.

First published by AuthorHouse 01/05/06

ISBN: 1-4208-9298-3(sc)

Library of Congress Control Number: 2005909750

Printed in the United States of America
Bloomington, Indiana

This book is printed on acid-free paper.

Cover painting by Stephen White, © 2005, courtesy of Stephen White & Village Smith Galleries
Cover Design by Sharon Hoglen
Cover photography by Dan Rossi

Dedicated to the memory of my brother, Tommy,

and

*to my friend, "o,"
who loves a good story*

Contents

Introduction xi
Thread Count 1
Autumnal Equinox 2
When I'm With You 4
Luncheon in Paris 5
Wisteria 6
The Belle of Bourbon Street 7
Stringing Beans 9
Astrid 10
Who Remains Nameless 11
El Paso 12
Sedition 13
Woman by the Savannah River 14
Aftermath 15
Ode to My Feet 16
Brilliant Delusion 18
Watchtower 19
Phantom of the Opera 20
Young Love 21
Storm Shelter 22
Frozen 23
Nightfall in Västerås 24
Death 25
Narcille 26

The Dance	27
Wave of the Future	28
My Kitchen	29
Separation	30
Agoraphobic	31
Saturday Morning	33
The Harvest	34
Too Close for Comfort	35
Walk in Central Park	36
Grandma's Fair-Haired Boy	38
Parabola	40
The Middle Ages	41
The Offering	42
Pier Fishing	43
Eventuality	44
Spartan	45
Open Door Policy	46
Rain	48
Chain of Fools	50
Vigil	51
Brown Dress	52
Last Laugh	53
Impossible Dream	54
Miss Willa Lee	55
You	56
Lament of a Beautiful Woman	57
Kommós	58

Cassiopeia	59
Preparing for Battle	60
Blackberry Picking	61
The Call	62
Supplication	63
Concerto	64
Birdsong	65
In Memoriam	66
Just Watch Me	68
Office Slave	69
Alpha to Omega	71
Ritual	72
Traveling Light	73
Surrender	74
Happiness	75
Vignette	77
Strawberries	78
Dulce Melos	79
Odalisque	80
Eating Watermelon in Granddaddy's Back Yard	81
Discarded Things	83
Torre Guelfa	84
Snake	85
Man in the Metro Station	86
Cutting Loose	87
Jack of Hearts	88
Hsi Ling Shi	90

Fair Divided Excellence	91
Fourth of July in Lewisville Square	92
The Comforter	93
Moon Flowers	94
A Clash of Vikings	95
Sweet Dreams	96
Meeting Rita Dove	97
Family Reunion at Lake Mälaren	98
Grief	99
Pillow Lava	100
Waiting Up	101
The New Me	102
Tommy	103
Resort	104
The Furies	105
Moonlighting	106
Night Nurse	107
Beach House	108
Casting the Second Stone	109
Going Nowhere	110
Mid-Summer of My Childhood, 1965	111
Hummingbirds	112
Kingston Mines (Chicago, 2003)	113
Love	114
Play Ball	115

Introduction

What I love most about writing poetry is the challenge of using words as threads, connecting the poet to the reader. In my view, a good poem works like a mirror, reflecting "colors" and images with such clarity that readers will say, "I know what it means to me." In other words, the point is not for you to find the poet in the poems, but for you to find yourself.

A few years ago, I attended a poetry reading accompanied by a close friend, visual artist Debrah Jean. The poet was Rita Dove, and I was completely enthralled with her strong voice and obvious love for words. That evening reminded me of my own long-dormant passion for words, language and poetry. So—I resolved to do something about it. *Thread Count* is the result.

I hope your experience of these poems will be for you, the reader, as real and true as writing them was for me.

Terri Kirby Erickson
September, 2005

MAY 1963

Thread Count

My mother hung wet sheets to dry from a rope
that stretched between two poles in our back yard, her motions
smooth and rhythmic as a synchronized swimmer. She
stooped and straightened again and again, her hands
moving across the line faster than
squirrels on telephone wire.

From my perch on the swing, I watched her work,
pumping my legs until I touched puffy
white clouds with the toes of my shoes, the squeak

of the metal chain steady as a metronome.
My body felt light as dandelion seeds, floating.
Higher and higher I swung, until it seemed
I was a kite soaring on the end of a

string. I slung my head back and let
my hair trail in the dirt, closing my eyes so the
sensation in my belly was like the swift

descent of an elevator in a tall building. The sun
felt like warm maple syrup dripping on my
face, and the air smelled of honeysuckle and bacon
grease in glass jars sitting on the window

sill. I opened my eyes as my mother lifted
the last sheet from the pile, with light illuminating the
threads like the hours in a child's summer day,
too many to count.

Autumnal Equinox

There is some sense when
autumn begins,
that the world is being
smothered by a colorful blanket.
Trees lose their emerald
radiance, the edges of their
leaves turn yellow, orange
or scarlet. Days grow shorter
and shadows
linger; the nights come
with a chill like bathwater
left in the tub too long.
Flowers that bloomed in lush
profusion on my front
porch, droop like tired children
fighting sleep. Vidalia onions

and garden tomatoes disappear
from grocery store shelves,
replaced by pumpkins and oddly
shaped squash.

When autumn arrives, winter is
only a frozen breath away,
bringing cold
and slush, runny noses and hacking
coughs, gray mornings and
twilight afternoons. It is the season

that swallows summer like
it never was—as if young girls in
sundresses were never kissed
in the moonlight, or
baseballs never soared
over a fence. There were no barbecues
or mosquito bites, sandals filled

with sand on the deck. Autumn
shakes the summer from
our minds until it falls like leaves,
skittering down an empty street.

When I'm With You

it's like I'm eight years old sitting in the back
of a moving car, my feet hanging out the window

with the hot wind blowing my toes and
shimmying up my legs and face and tangling my
hair. There's a cooler in the trunk filled with

fried chicken, deviled eggs and fresh tomato
sandwiches slathered with mayonnaise and bottles
of Orange Crush hidden under the ice. We'll stop
for lunch halfway to the beach,
too soon to smell the
salt in the air but close enough to imagine it.

There's a blue bucket with a yellow
shovel that I can't keep from touching

and a shower curtain smell of inflatable
rafts folded in a paper bag on the floorboard.
The people I love most are with me

so the world is safe as a blanket tucked
under my chin and happiness is something
I expect, like birthday cake.

Luncheon in Paris

It looked like a celebration, but perhaps they celebrated
every day,
she in her red beret, he in his black cap.
They had a feast of soufflés
from entrée to dessert,
as if they would rather dine on air,

but chose a clever substitute. Every so often he stroked
her cheek or took her hand.
She laughed with her head thrown
back and throat exposed, akin to a young girl,
flirting. They spoke like conspirators

with no desire to spoil the surprise for anyone else.
And after they paid the check, he reached
for his cane, she took his arm,
and they strolled down the sidewalk of
the Rue de Castiglione like gracious owners of the property.

Wisteria

Indolent flowers, how
firmly your vines wrap
around a host, like the

arms of a jewel thief and
a woman wearing diamonds.
Your divine sense of

color, your heady scent,
are powerful arguments
for survival.

You fall like clusters of
grapes, your petals both
heavy and delicate,

like Sumo wrestlers
drinking tea from porcelain
cups. You are the perfect

distraction as your stem and
roots work their way into,
around, between, and

over everything in sight,
like cool, green lava,
with lavender ashes.

The Belle of Bourbon Street

She wore a purple feathered boa wrapped
around her shoulders and shoes so high, the
heels looked like a pair of stilts, and that walk,
well it was more like a sashay with attitude
so crowds on Bourbon Street parted like
she was God's hand on the Red Sea when
she passed by. The scent of her perfume
mingled with beignets and chicory coffee
and flowers lush as pregnant Tahitian
princesses. Chlotilde could work a sidewalk,

no doubt about it, and when she strolled
into a bar, the doors opened like magic
as the sound of clinking glasses and
near hysterical laughter and the crack
of a cue ball on the break spilled
into the street. Every stool had her
name on it so before she sat down, the
bartender parked a Tanqueray and tonic
with a chilled lime twist on a crystal
coaster. She smiled, thanked him,

and raised 'just what the doctor ordered'
to her lips while every man in the room
stopped what he was doing and watched.
Hours later, when the bar closed down
and Chlotilde's head was resting lightly
on her arms, the bartender placed a quiet
call to the Garden District. Fifteen
minutes on the button a black Rolls Royce
slid along the curb quiet as a cat in a
cathedral and out stepped a big man

in a dark jacket, his hair a gleaming halo
of silver. What few stragglers were left
knew better than to meet his eye when he
walked past. He put his hand on her
back and asked the bartender, "She get into
trouble tonight, Batiste?" and the bartender
shook his head, "No sir, Mr. Rabalais,
it was a good night," which he didn't
argue with although a good night would be
the one where his daughter stayed sober.

He lifted her like he'd done a thousand times
and carried her outside, that feather boa
dragging behind them like the tail of a comet.
"Daddy," she murmured, her arms tightening
around his neck. "Yes bébé, we goin' home
now," he said, as he laid her in the back seat
gentle as a gardenia in a corsage box. After the
car disappeared into a patch of fog rolling in from
the river, a young man on the corner bowed and
bid a silent farewell to the Belle of Bourbon Street.

Stringing Beans

There is a rhythm to stringing beans
like the kind of pace a runner sets after

miles down the road, when she
isn't thinking of running

anymore as a thing she's doing but a

thing she has become. With a bowl on
your lap and a paper sack brimming

with beans by your side, you reach and

snap, reach and snap, the brittle skin
breaking and the strings curling like green
ribbons. The mossy scent of their jade

juices shakes loose a memory of

diving into bushes and rolling in the grass,
when there was no bad back or stiff
shoulder, no clutching of rails or

gingerly stepping over stones.

But the crisp beans feel cool as emeralds
and the heavy bowl is a comforting
weight on your legs, anchoring you

somehow, to the moment, so that after
a while, that's all there is to it.

Astrid

On the sidewalks of Göteborg, this diminutive woman
somehow commands the pavement. With her stylish ensemble,
her regal bearing, and the way she wields

her cane like a scepter,
the blood of Swedish kings pales to canal water in
comparison to her impeccable breeding.

Her eyes, which conform to the crescent
shape of prominent cheek bones, miss nothing as
she moves through the crowds.

She ducks into a shop, admiring the vivid colors of a silk scarf.
She smiles because the "owner" is away, and
she can browse all she likes without

buying. Back in the throng,
she walks to a corner café where she orders porridge and a coffee,
braving an outdoor table despite a chill in the air.

She watches humanity surge before her in various
shapes and sizes, nodding to people she has encountered
on other outings. She lifts the coffee cup and thinks about

the perfection of a life she has carved with her own
hands, while a tourist snaps her picture, convinced he has
captured a queen in disguise.

Who Remains Nameless

I want to show you everything, the change purse I
wore on a chain when I was six, my
daughter's baby shoes, the
way the edges of my mouth blur when I cry. I want

to hurry a dream so I can wake and tell
you how it ended. I look over my
shoulder as if you are behind me, waiting to
hear the joke. I'd like to see

your first treasures, the arrowheads,
the bits of string, the copper penny crushed
flat on railroad tracks, to know
the things you treasure now.

Such thoughts, of course, are little girls
sitting on porch steps—listening for the car door,
the footfall, the lift and twirl of
greeting that will never

come. You remain unreachable as a pearl
of water trapped in gypsum.
There are too many layers wedged
between us, and you prefer your hiding place.

El Paso

Heat rises from streets and driveways
and up through the soles of your shoes
until your eyes are like panels of hot glass
through which every image is blurred and distorted.
Even the desert, with its parched, choking air
and vast, grainy hide punctured with cactus

plants and crawling with rattlesnakes,
shimmers in the distance like a photograph

melting slowly on a pyre. The mountains
loom like craggy faces of cowboy
ancestors who never left the rocky range,

under a sky so wide and blue, it could be
be the ocean shaken, not stirred, like a bone
dry martini. The cork-like scent of tortillas
mingles with horseflesh and leather, and

the smell of your own skin, baking under a
fine layer of sand like salted meat on a
grill. Yet there is stark beauty in the
landscape of this sun-blasted bit of earth,
like bare, bleached bones, picked clean of decay.
It is a place of grit and endurance,

where the arc of a man's arm whipping
over his head and the strength of his legs
gripping the haunches of an angry bull,

becomes a symbol for hanging on when
everything inside him screams, let go.

Sedition

You there, the sullen, black-clad girl
with the tattoo and pierced belly,
the metal stud that clacks on your teeth
and rests on your tongue like a beetle, where
did you hide my beautiful baby? Is she
somewhere inside this strange carapace
waiting to be reborn?

Will she emerge with her milk-sodden chins
and somnolent smile? Will she laugh at leaves
kicked in the air, lift her dimpled hand to pat
my cheek, love her mother best? Time passes
like loops in a roller coaster and never goes
backward, until the name we crooned in the night
belongs to someone we scarcely

recognize, someone who has drawn a line
in the sand we dare not cross, or lose
her entirely.

Woman by the Savannah River

Every day she sat by the river, heat taking her breath
like a cat in a crib. The cloying clutch of sticky air
pasted her blouse to her thin body, revealing
ribs reminiscent of archeological finds with their
dearth of flesh. Her eyes were liquid and brown

as chocolate melting in its wrapper, fixed on
passersby as if she knew them well, or knew their kind,
and it wasn't as nice as they liked to believe.

She was no particular age, or all of them at once; it
was impossible to discern. Her hair was black as a
moonless sky, her skin translucent as rice paper. Some days
she muttered under her breath, Bible verses or curses,
no one could say. Other days she was quiet like a

fortress after battle, when everyone inside was dead or gone.
She never begged, but wouldn't turn down a donation

snatched from your hand before you were sure
what you had given. She tucked it into the folds of her
voluminous skirt, which ballooned around her like a giant

blossom on a slim stalk, and whispered what sounded
like *Merci,*

but it might have been mercy, more for us than for
herself, who seemed to want nothing.

She sat in the same spot until the sun dipped into the
water like a hot fist in a copper cistern, and then
disappeared to wherever street people go at night—perhaps
changing into crows, invisible in the dark.

Aftermath

Such innocence between
anticipation and
disappointment, a pale

expanse of yielding flesh,
an indrawn breath,
the impossibility of discerning
what to hope for.
Your heart is a white rabbit
pulled suddenly

from a hat, quivering in the chill
air. There is no vulnerability
like this, no dreams of being
naked in a classroom compare. You
are like a baby torn

from the womb, slapped and laid
screaming on a cold table. There
is no mercy in the end,
no bough in which your cradle rests.
You are left with nothing,

not even a note pinned to your
collar, pleading
for someone else to love you.

Ode to My Feet

I am crazy about
my feet, each little
digit as
dear to me as ten
of my best

friends. I love the
way none of my
toes touch when I'm
barefoot, as if
they are a healthy family
who know the meaning
of boundaries, and
how they band
together as
a team inside a
torturing shoe.
The nails

are like an
artist's canvas,
waiting to reflect
my whim
of color—
innocent pink,
sophisticated coral,
passionate

crimson. I adore the smooth
arc of my instep,
the soft skin at
the apex of the

curve. My feet connect
my body to
the earth and
carry me wherever
I wish to

go. They fit just so
in a lover's palm, and on
the pedals of my

bicycle. They are the
perfect tango
partners.

The best part is,
they belong to me.

Brilliant Delusion

There is something magical about lamps
on a screened-in porch,
the amber glow beneath a hand-sewn shade,
the graceful flare

of fabric directing the beams. Lamps
illuminate this human
foray into the outdoors when
other creatures must rely on the
mercurial moon. Secure in our protective illusion
of mesh, we
enjoy the night air without
the bother of insects. We lock

the flimsy door against intruders, creating a chimera
of security. Yet it is
the light more than anything else, like campfires
dotting the open plains, that

quiets our fears. Perhaps animals are smarter,
understanding
that nothing holds back the darkness

of deadly intent. They crouch in the bushes and hide
in the trees, while we play cards and dance
and laugh out loud, pretending
we are invincible in our radiant cocoons.

Watchtower

She wears the same skirt every day for a week, never mind
that it's splattered with yolk and stained with coffee; no one
sees her. Dish towels hang limply from their pegs in the

kitchen like a line of disconsolate shepherds, their faces
concealed in the folds of their robes. Sweet breads lay
frozen in plastic wrappers in the freezer, ready for
company that never comes. Delicate porcelain cups and

saucers handed down for generations gather dust in
the china cabinet. Photographs from happier days are

scattered from room to room like bread crumbs leading
to her past. Her husband, long dead, smiles at her from his
metal frame. They never wanted children, complete in

each other they said, and now she is alone. At ninety-one, she
cloisters herself in this apartment, where she has lived

half her life. She orders everything on the telephone, her needs
simple—a tin of crackers, a wheel of cheese, a basket of fruit.
Each afternoon as shadows lengthen across the room, she sits
in the same wing-backed chair beneath the same

painting of a flock of birds skimming across a lake, taking in
a view that has become a painting in itself with its constancy. She

can hear the air moving in and out of her ancient lungs,
the ticking of the clock on the mantle, the settling of timbers

in the ceiling. She avoids the gilt mirror that hangs over the end
table. The creature who stares back is a gnome in a folk tale
remembered from childhood, not the sleek, satiny
woman who took so much for granted, who believed
such powerful flesh would never fail her.

Phantom of the Opera

My best friend's father had spells of taking
to his couch with a glass of bourbon
on the rocks and a Puccini
opera on the stereo, turned loud
enough to vibrate the roof tiles. I was ten years
old so I didn't know it was bourbon at
the time, only that it didn't come in the exotic
colors of children's
drinks—bright red, purple, orange—
and he swirled it around and around
in the glass before
sipping, as if he might change his mind.
Madame Butterfly and *Tosca,*
La Boheme and *Turandot* were the musical
backdrops to our games;
the weight of his
melancholy hanging over us like a funeral
tent, though we could not define it.
Sadness was too abstract, grief impossible
to imagine, and a man laid out
full length in the middle of the day,
his arm over his face, a glass
on his chest as if his heart was
a table, was a riddle we
could not solve. So we tip-toed around
his still form, and held our laughter until
the door slammed behind us.
Instinctively, we did not laugh at
him, or even speak of it,
understanding as small animals will—
some things are best left alone.

Young Love

In the back of an old Buick, no doubt driven by
his older brother, a young boy of perhaps fourteen sits beside
a girl of the same age. They are framed in the rear wind

shield as we stop for traffic.
She has long, black hair that cascades down her pale
neck like Nile water. His hand is disproportionately
large compared to his slender arm,
like the paw of a newborn St. Bernard,

and cupped gently around her head. His palm fits her
crown close as a prayer cap, and he stares at

her profile, spellbound. There may never be
another sight that moves him quite the
same way as the soft curve of her mouth,
the slight bump on the bridge of her nose, the dark
fan of lashes on her plump cheek. He may close his eyes
one day, years from this moment,

and feel her head beneath his hand again, round and
hard as a Granny Smith apple—and think to himself,
nothing has ever come close to this ecstasy.

Storm Shelter

It wasn't so much that I was afraid of storms, but that
the people around me were afraid for me. My grandmother
used to wear out the carpet pacing back and forth while jagged

lightning bolts cut the sky, bleeding flashes of fluorescent blue
across the walls like strobe lighting in a dance club.
She hated thunder most, that harmless bluster that rumbles in low,
throaty octaves favored by mating alligators and ornery
old men. My mother warned my brother and me

to stay away from windows, to sit quietly on the couch in the
living room in case lightning struck the house and
rolled around the baseboards like errant

cannon balls. So I perceived some danger if not actually taking it in
because I was a child who appreciated a passionate display,
particularly if I could view it from afar.

Of course, my obligation as a toy owner was to ensure their safety
as well as my own, and I would hastily grab handfuls of dolls
and assorted stuffed wildlife and line them up on the

sofa. Between them and under them, my poor
brother and I would sit waiting for the storm to pass,

his docile acceptance of this ritual rather surprising, but no
doubt I was insistent and he was after all, shorter at the time.
It was the kind of shelter which I have yet to duplicate in my
adult life, as lightning cracks around the ones I love with
alarming regularity, and there is nothing I can do to save them.

Frozen

A shoulder turned away in the night
is like a wall of ice. I clench my
jaw to keep my teeth from chattering,
draw the blanket closer around

me. The things we never speak of are
like detritus in a sagging gutter. It is a
weight that pulls us down, but
we never say the words

that might save us. A chasm yawns
between your side and mine, filled with
dark and indiscernible shapes, like
furniture in an unfamiliar

room. Yet, once there was a boy with
your name, who slept lightly in a
single bed, whose mother
kissed his cheek and

swept the hair from his forehead. If
only I had known him, could
see that he survives in you,
and believe that

somewhere in your fortress, is the
memory of tenderness.

Nightfall in Västerås

In a cottage surrounded by fragrant lilies-of-the-valley and forget-me-nots, an elderly man stokes a small fire in the grate, while his wife of fifty years curls with a book in her favorite

chair. She glances up now and then to rest her eyes from the page, and the view from the window is a lilac bush in full bloom, and the blue haze of a twilight that will scarcely dim before the

sun rises again. The fire casts a warm glow over the room, illuminating photographs of children and grandchildren, books crowding every available space, a plate of half-eaten

cheese and hard tack on the coffee table. A light rain begins to patter against the roof as her husband rises from the hearth. Tomorrow he will chop more wood, and she will take a walk by

the lake, grateful that she can still amble about with her stiff knee. Tonight, however, they will turn off the lamps, crawl under soft eiderdown, and sleep until the nightingale sings in the morning.

Death

Death is stealthy, like ninja
with a better wardrobe.
No need for all that basic black

when so often souls waiting to
be snatched are bathed in light,
surrounded by wildflowers

and butterflies, having a picnic. How
silly would it look then, to be
swathed in somber clothes, creeping

about like a night crawler? It likes
to come upon you when you
least expect, blending in, so to speak,

with the scenery. It is familiar with
idle gossip, how to stand
unobtrusively, holding a wine

glass. It waits until your eye
is off the ball and takes it, just like
that—your child, your husband,

your friend—as if casually strolling
across the lawn in a quiet
game of croquet.

Narcille

"Baby, it is hell getting old," she said,
taking a break from the oven, a rack
of freshly baked rum balls, heavy on the
rum, cooling. On the other end of the
line, I smiled, imagining her expressive
face, her large body somehow light and
airy as meringues, the honeyed aromas
of her compact kitchen. Narcille never
married, a fact she attributed to a boy who
mysteriously disappeared—from her life
or the world at large, I never inquired.
Some things aren't meant for conversation.
But being young, I believed everyone
should be in love, even cantankerous Cajun
candy-makers, so I invented the Captain.
He was away at sea, but constantly missing
his beloved, whom he was too shy to write
directly. He sent his missives to me, the
story went, to share with her, which I did.
"The Captain is in Singapore," I said.
"He bought an ivory comb for your hair."
Or, "the Captain is in Marseilles, longing
to drink champagne from your shoe."
And she would reply, "Go on with your
monkeyshines," but her eyes would sparkle
and her face glow softly, as if my words
conjured up the innocent girl whose love
was not lost but merely at sea. So, with
feigned nonchalance, she continued our
conversation by asking, "Where is the
Captain tonight?" as twilight settled on
her house like a mauve evening jacket.

The Dance

It was a dance to one song,
your palm warm and firm against the curve
of my back, my cheek grazing the fabric
of your coat. The singer crooned a ballad of such
longing that tears quivered
in her eyelashes,

and your heart
beat against me like
a fist on a door. The moon was brilliant in
the night sky, with a scrim of

wispy clouds that moved like black lace
slipping from a bare shoulder,
while your breath teased my ear like an ocean
breeze, hiding its salty secrets in a

conch shell. But even as we danced, it was
ending—like the lid closing slowly on a music box,
as if the moon was a magician's coin that
vanished up a sleeve, and the dance,
strangers pressed too close in
a crowd.

Wave of the Future

A road was wide as the Mississippi between a black child
and a white, living on opposite sides in 1962. (Why,

mamas would sooner their babies pick up a rattlesnake than
traverse that Great Divide!) We stood at the curb, both

five years old or thereabouts with baby dolls in the crooks of our
arms, our eyes linked like rosary beads. One day she was through with

staring and crossed the street, just like that. We smiled, joined hands and
started walking. We were two girls, out for a stroll. It didn't occur

to us that we were problematic, even with people gaping and pointing
like we were carrying stolen property. I can still feel her palm,

soft as butter, and the hot asphalt under our patent leather
shoes as we strode toward the future unafraid, like prophets.

My Kitchen

I picture my heart as a stainless steel kitchen,
with gleaming pots and spotless pans, where
the sink reflects my face when bending over it
to wash my hands.

There is nothing soft here, no artfully stitched
towels or throw rugs, no frilly curtains or oven mitts.
Every surface is hard and shiny and new; and
each piece fits.

No cracks or crevices where something might seep
in, no basket for a cat to curl up and sleep, no windows
for neighbors to peer inside, no place at all
where love can hide.

Separation

To leave you standing, framed in the doorway,
your face as familiar to me as
the moon in the sky, is like wandering
outside my own skin.
Your body was the branch in the current, without
which I might have drowned
a thousand times.
The sound of your breathing was

the music of my sleep. We are linked in silent
collusion, the only two people
on earth who carry the memory
of us, and the pain of this parting.

Our hands lift to wave good-bye like white
flags on a battlefield, raised by soldiers
who have lost their taste for war.

Agoraphobic

Lillian sat near a window by necessity
because the room had so many of them, they
could not be avoided. She was brushing her

hair, the glossy ringlets bouncing like
bungee cords dangling from a bridge.
The monotonous drone of a lawn

mower mingled with the blare
of music from an ice cream truck rattling
down the street were the persistent

sounds that worked their way under the
narrow gap between sill and glass. Bees
occasionally missed their marks

and hit the screen, leaving pollen dust in
bright circles like multiple suns. If she turned
her head, she could see flashes of color as the

neighbors' children ran back and forth through
the sprinkler in their yard. Despite all this
evidence that she was connected to

a larger world, there was only the feel
of the brush in her hand, and the tug of
her scalp with each stroke. Lillian

had long since escaped from the
ambiguities and consternations of
life outside her house. Civilization

in its tumultuous intensity frightened
her to such extremes that she could
literally feel herself imploding when

exposed to it. When she was most
stricken by the feeling that there was no
air to be found, that her legs would

give way any moment and she would fall
to the floor gasping, she would quickly leave
wherever she was, whatever she was doing,

often abandoning the clothes she had
intended to buy, the roast at the meat counter,
the person with whom she was having lunch,

and hurtle home like it was the last
haven in a city set ablaze. Eventually, she
decided that home was the only place

she felt safe and there was no reason
to leave it again. Her husband had little
patience with her "eccentricity," and would

probably divorce her some day unless innate
laziness prevented him from deviating from his
own patterns. Her friends had finally

given up their urgent coaxing for her to attend
their social gatherings, or to "see someone"
professionally. Meanwhile, she had

recently decided that the house was
entirely too large for her purposes and
the bedroom was the only possible refuge.

If the bedroom became too much for her,
she imagined rolling into a tiny
ball and shutting herself in a drawer,

but in the meantime, she brushed her hair
incessantly and daydreamed of other
fearless lives, where she found the cure

for cancer, searched for rare butterflies in the
Brazilian rainforest, or was able to open
the front door to get the newspaper.

Saturday Morning

Ham and eggs fry in a skillet
while Granddaddy sings and the

sun pours through frilly curtains,
starched and still as nosy neighbors

listening by the window. Sitting
around the kitchen table with

its vinyl tablecloth and covered
toaster, dipping white bread

in lukewarm coffee, it's hard for
children not to giggle and act up

with their grandmother smiling so
sweet like a lady behind a counter,

like somebody they see all the time
but never talk to, and granddaddy

wearing an apron, making breakfast
and trying to be normal enough for two.

The Harvest

On the side of Valhallavägen, a little girl
stoops to pick
dandelions. Her hair catches

the light like
a prism as she reaches again and again for the bright
tufts of yellow on their thin stalks.

Her parents chat idly with friends on the corner
while cars cruise by slowly, admiring the
architecture of the

buildings and the fresh faces
of cyclists whizzing past
them near the curb. The air is crisp as the fold

of a linen tablecloth,
and the sky clear and sparkling as a water goblet.
The child, absorbed in her task,

sees nothing
but the golden flowers she has gathered,
and those waiting for her to find them.

Too Close for Comfort

His skin burned black as
a Nubiana plum,
a man crouched in the median
holding a
cardboard sign. Streaks of sweat
ran down his face like a
glass of cold beer on a wooden

bar. His very stillness drew
the attention of
motorists the way his pacing,
chattering brethren, (the ones who
usually commanded this patch

of cement), did not. In purple
crayon, he had written,

"Homeless.

Will eat apples for
dessert. Did you know there
are 2,000 kinds of apples?"

People drove by slowly,
but kept their windows rolled
tight, wondering
how a man who likes apples
fell so far from the cart.

Walk in Central Park

It is snowing in Central Park,
each flake puffy as a poodle emerging
from a salon. I am wearing red
mittens; you have
a striped scarf.

The scene is picturesque as
a postcard, the gently rolling drifts, the crust
of ice along the lane
stiff as pilgrim
collars.

Still, we walk in silence,
our crystalline breath like the collective
sighs of angels, the color of
christening
gowns.

Our feet crunch salt
strewn over a bridge, the preferred
condiment for spicing winter
roads. It is a sound
like hearts

breaking, the crush of glass under
a tire. Crossing the Great Lawn, your hip
grazes mine—by accident,
of course.
The days

when your touch was deliberate
have long passed. How ironic that the two of us,
so heavy with words
unsaid, are
treading

through this plain of snow,
leaving footprints deep as caverns
in a substance
of maximum
lightness.

Grandma's Fair-Haired Boy

He had curly blond hair and blue
eyes, she said, kneading bread dough
and wiping the sweat off her
brow with the back of her arm. After

school, he'd ride his bicycle to my
house and we would walk a while.
What happened to him is what
we wanted to know, but all she said

was that his parents were rich
and they sent him away, as if telling
that much explained the rest—why
they never saw each other again,
why she married our red-faced, balding

grandfather. Of course
she must have loved him since
they had four children and lived together
longer than we'd all been alive,
but she never got that look
on her face when she talked about

him. She showed us a picture of that
boy one afternoon, the only one she had.
We didn't think much of it, but she
lifted it from the box like a baby

from a bassinette. After all, we thought,
what kind of person would leave her?
She was the best cook ever born and
and you could tell her anything
like she was your best friend in the

world, which she probably was. We pretty
much agreed we'd like to punch
his lights out, but living without her
chocolate pound cake, in our view,
was punishment enough.

Parabola

Be open to possibility,
no matter what the
cost. Not to
fold in, but
to fan
out,
is a
life
well
lived.
It isn't the
lob, but the
smooth arc of the
landing that counts.

The Middle Ages

I've just read a book where the baby-faced author
used the term, "middle-aged woman," over and over
again to describe various characters, but no one
important. I had thought old age was the magic
cloak of invisibility for women, but perhaps
it begins now—when my generous brown

hair makes room for streaks of gray, when my chin
sags comfortably into my neck when I'm reading,

as if relaxing in a favorite chair—and my hips flare
ever so slightly beyond the space they once occupied,
beneath a canopy of soft belly. But it's alright
with me, these subtle changes, because I'm

more settled in my body now, as if it finally feels
like home, and my thoughts range over the whole
world like those dreams where you are flying. It
seems impossible that anyone could toss the words

"middle-aged woman" so indifferently into a story,
as if she is an affront to decent society simply by
having to be mentioned, as if she ought to slink off
the page like a bad dog, cowering. Well, I refuse to
be banished when I've come into myself so

beautifully, after spending so much of my life
slightly numb, like a crossed leg. I feel everything

these days, but it doesn't scare me like it used
to, doesn't make me want to burrow into
someone else like a chigger. I can be alone now
and if that's what being a middle-aged
woman means, it was worth the wait.

The Offering

Gardenias floating in a crystal bowl, rested on
the table beside her reading chair. White

as wedding dresses, they were both lush and
innocent, like ladies at their first Cotillion. She

smiled softly, appreciating the kind gesture, this
fragrant gift that spoke for itself without fanfare.

He knew she loved them, and simply placed
them where she would spend some portion of

her day. There had been men in her life whose
effusive language filled page after page with

flowery deceit, every word like a separate entry
in its own beauty pageant. She was nothing

more than an audience, someone to applaud
their verbal agility. How gaudy such opulent

displays seemed when compared to this humble
offering, holy and honorable as an altar bouquet.

Pier Fishing

Sitting on a hard wooden bench with a
hundred splinters waiting for the brush
of your hand, watching the dip and sway

of fishing poles as waves undulate beneath
the pier and foam around the pilings in
patterns intricate as Milanese lace, the smell

of shrimp hulls, fish heads, and cooking
grease wafting on a breeze of scorched air, the
vibration of the boards as people stroll up

and down, peeking into everybody's bucket
to see if they're "catching anything." Girls in
bikinis, their skin burnished gold and

gleaming with suntan oil and their escorts
burgeoning with muscles like newly stuffed
Boudin sausages, old married couples

hand-in-hand, their steps in practiced syncopation,
children squealing and darting from side to side,
trailing drops of ice cream and scaring their

parents who spot too many hazards to count,
but the best part is the frantic nibble on the end
of your line, the jerk of the rod and the reeling in,

the thrill of knowing that whatever has taken the bait
will be revealed as soon as it clears the water and
if it should be a fish and not a piece of seaweed,

a sea snake, a crab, a boot, or a shell, you will feel
like a conqueror for that brief moment before you
gently remove the hook and toss it back in the ocean.

Eventuality

Your words drop like
coins in my palm,

the sound of champagne
glasses clinking.

To meet your gaze is impossible.
There is only the shine

of these perfect discs, the
hypnotic pull of their luster.

Cool against
my fevered skin, they are the

tangible reality. Don't tell
me, please,

what they are worth—this
unfamiliar currency.

The emptiness in my hand
when you take

them back,
will be loss enough.

Spartan

On my knees, knocked from my bicycle,
rocks embedded in my flesh like cloves on a
Christmas ham,
I am too proud

to cry. To think a child would have
such mastery at the sight of her own blood,
could rise like a Phoenix and pretend it didn't

hurt. I remember
taking off like a shot for home, my legs
streaked red, my hair flapping behind me like

streamers. She lives in me, this fierce warrior,
this pygmy Amazon
who won't shed a tear without the

curtains closed tight, who
believes that pain is private, like prayer.

Open Door Policy

The old man sat quiet in a chair near the open door,
his gnarled hands resting in his lap, still and calm
as well water. A dog lay curled at his feet
on the worn carpet of an old trailer that had seen
better days but was neat and clean
with everything just so, the way
he liked it. Every day he sat near that open

door, watching cars go by, and the children
playing in the yard across the street,
their squeals of laughter
like music in his head that was better

than choirs in heaven, or so he believed. Jesus
was a big one for loving little children and the old
man agreed with his philosophies
on that score. He had two sons of his own
and every now and then one of them

dropped by with a pan of cornbread or a magazine
that he could read sharp as when he
was a boy, his vision still perfect with the

silver-framed glasses that perched on the end of
his long nose. It was a fine nose, aristocratic
somebody once said, even if the rest of his face
looked like a pitted
plum, round and florid and plain as home cooking.
He didn't think anything of it when the boys busted

through the door (neither one of them
much older than his dog there on the floor),

since he was partial to company, that being
one of reasons for his open door
policy along with taking in the sights. When they

grabbed him and started beating him on the head, it was
like being under water where
everything moves too slow and all the sounds
on the surface are muffled. When
he came to, his wallet was gone and he couldn't find
his way to the telephone. It seemed like

all he could make out was light and shadow.
The doctor said his vision
wouldn't come back, which seemed like
a shame when
it was so sharp and clear before, and his sons
kept going on about locking the front
door from now on. Well, he kept

the door open anyway, being too old to change his ways,
he said. Even if he couldn't watch the children,
he could hear their laughter and imagine

them running through the tall grass, and he
could feel the rumble of cars going by
and the breeze on his face. He would have given
them boys all the money in his wallet if they'd
asked for it. His needs were few
and simple, but he sure missed
his sight, yes he did.

Rain

Rain is made of whispers
and sighs, the exhalation of
heavenly creatures

who peer at us from the
clouds. Each droplet makes
its way from the sky, leaping

like acrobats in silver
leotards, landing nimbly and
gracefully on leaves

and blossoms and the upturned
faces of little children who
have no makeup to

run, or hairdos to ruin. It pools
in low lying places,
colors gathering

at the edges in rainbow
hues; it sinks into the ground,
nourishing seeds

and plants and tiny insects
whose thirst exceeds
their fear of

drowning. It is music
for lovers, a lullaby for babies
cozy in their cradles.

Rain strokes the earth until
it resembles
an Impressionist painting,

until it gives way its indurate
shell and lies open
and soft as a woman's palm.

Chain of Fools

There is a woman waiting
in a stone cottage by an azure sea,
gazing through an open
window.
Gauzy curtains blow
inward, and tiny grains

of sand and salt dot her skin.
The floor is bare wood, the walls
painted white. She
hears a wind
chime of shells tinkling, the cry
of gulls, the breaking

of waves on the shore—but never
a human voice save her own.
She knows he is not coming back,
that he has built a
hundred dwellings like this
one, all over the

world. It is a trail of sorrow,
a chain of solitary lighthouse
keepers, a necklace of
black pearls adorning
the throat of
his latest conquest.

Vigil

A mother stands silent in a doorway, alert as
a bird on a branch, keeping her nest in

sight. Her children lie sleeping, vulnerable
and unaware as robin's eggs, their rosy

lips parted as milky breath fills the room like
steam from a farmer's pail. Their skin, soft as

peonies, glows like goose down under a streak
of lamplight spilling across their beds. Their

chests rise and fall, lifting the snaps of their
cotton pajamas, the covers kicked away no

sooner than she tucks them in. Still, she lingers,
listening to the music of their sighs, the sweet

sonata of her children breathing, while the
world circles the house like a hungry beast.

Brown Dress

When I was a little girl,
I wanted to wear the same dress
every day. It was brown plaid
with a scalloped collar and a sash
that tied around the waist. (My legs were
whippet thin and my shoes were like

an undertow, pulling at my
socks). I wore it climbing trees,
digging graves for dead birds
and standing, properly attired,
as their solitary mourner.
I dripped fudge sickle on

it and the stain never showed.
I ran without impediment,
walked with a regal step, caught
lightning bugs in a glass jar, skipped rope,
swung so high the chains nearly
looped around the bar, visited

my grandmother on Sunday afternoons.
I wore it until it was nothing more than
brown threads and tattered edges, until
my mother brought home a yellow,
dotted Swiss bathing suit with a
ruffled bottom. I shifted loyalty, wondering

what the boy next door would think of that.

Last Laugh

I feel so heavy,
like rolled carpet.
My body flops

in the chair, my
arms and legs
useless and stiff.

If I could move,
I'd break the mirrors,
every one, so I

couldn't see the
pain up close.
This pinched,

wan face, eyes
big as flying saucers,
the trembling

lip—I've seen it
all before
and it disgusts

me. If another man
says I love you
and he isn't

my father, I might
laugh myself
to death.

Impossible Dream

There is a house in my mind, white clapboard with a wrap-around porch. Flowers spill in copious profusion from hanging baskets and ceramic urns, their petals moist with dew. Nestled against the cushions of an antique glider, a child lays her head in her mother's lap as she reads a story filled with fairy queens and good deeds and magical animals with kind eyes. At her feet

are two little boys, their faces rapt, their spirits yearning for bold adventure in the way of those whose place in the world is secure. Just inside the front door, a cat warmed by a shaft of sunlight lies sleeping in a chair, dreaming of cream in a deep bowl. In the kitchen are curls of apple peels on the sideboard, and the exotic scent of cinnamon and cloves wafting from the oven. Upstairs,

the beds are made and the bathrooms cleaned. Toys and crayons and books are scattered here and there, because it is home and not a showplace. Across town, there is a man who carries this house and these people in his heart every moment of every day, thinking of the evening as it might unfold. His children will be waiting for him at the edge of the yard, their features

alive with anticipation. As he pulls into the driveway and opens the car door, they leap at him like puppies, the sound of their laughter like bubbles rising in a champagne glass. He will gather them in his arms all at once, while his gaze searches the porch steps for the beloved face and figure of his wife. She is always there, lovely and fragrant as night blooming

orchids. Tonight, he will wash her hair after the children are in bed, a ritual she adores. He imagines the weight of it in his hands, the soft sigh as she gives herself to the moment utterly, with the trust of a child. Afterwards, they will walk through the house holding hands, turning off the lamps one by one, the murmur of their voices a lullaby that sings their babies to sleep.

Miss Willa Lee

Willa Lee was a languorous swoon
of a woman,
always on the verge
of wilting like lettuce, or dropping

to the ground, heavy as a feather dipped
in molasses. She drank pink
lemonade from a
Spode Virginia teacup, and

carried a Battenburg lace handkerchief.
Her fair skin blanched at the
slightest hint of unguarded
emotion so admirers

spoke with hushed tones, as if in line
to view the
remains. She moved in tiny,
mincing steps like a Chinese girl

with bound feet. Men walked
beside her with their arms outstretched,
in case she toppled over. They
swear it was the cut

of her eyes under thick lashes,
like pieces of bottle green glass,
that made them yearn
to break her fall.

You

You are a comet which fell
burning into
my heart, a lick of flame in its
tail that ignited my skin from the inside

out. There is no cessation of the heat
that surges through my veins, no respite
from the longing that assails me.

There is only this fevered thrashing in
an empty bed, your letter glowing
on the nightstand
like a Japanese lantern.

Lament of a Beautiful Woman

How fragile we are, women on the waning side of beauty,
offering up our final bouquets, the tops of

our breasts exposed in evening gowns like meringues
on a platter. We catch sight of ourselves in a glass

and turn away quickly, lest this brief glimpse glean
more than we can bear to interpret as self.

We are complimented with those fatal words,
"You look good for your age," a line that cuts like a

Samurai sword across our frail egos. It was only moments
ago that we emerged from years of insecurity into

the full realization of our power, meeting every gaze
with utter confidence and aplomb. How glorious to be desired,

courted, won, and even cast aside in the end, which left
telltale traces of sadness in our eyes, a look few men can resist.

And then, like a thief on a bicycle, time steals what
we have taken for granted, what we have counted on,

what we believed would never desert us—and we are left
with mere vestiges of our vanished youth.

It is only in certain light, on days when we have had
enough rest, when we angle our faces a particular

way, that a trace of lost loveliness returns to us, like
the faint scent of perfume lingering on a pillowcase.

Kommós

I have lost track of who is locked in, who is locked
out. There is only this door and my feeble cries and my
impassioned entreaties. Lassitude steals

over me like a tide, swirling and bubbling
around me like foam. My neck is weary of its frail
support; my heavy head leans into

the wood as my fingers trace the grain.
I have come undone here, undone. There is
the memory of you peeling my heart

like a plum, the rich scent of fruit
in the air and your hands like farmer's hands
measuring the harvest. The heat of you cannot reach

me here, the timbre of your voice a distant
sound like chapel bells, calling us to pray. We sit
alone in the dark, our broken

wings like paper kites tangled in
tree branches, forgetting how it
felt to fly.

Cassiopeia

Doomed to hang upside
down like a broken
umbrella, Cassiopeia

circles the cosmos. She is
eternally seated at her
vanity, combing

her hair—all for
a simple boast. If such
punishment was

meted out daily, the sky
would be littered
with more chairs than

Versailles, and the earth
a barren reflection
in a billion mirrors.

Preparing for Battle

You are implacable, hard as stone.
Such rigidity is called "strong" in men,
as if your silence lifted weights,
its muscles bulging like overstuffed
easy chairs. If only I could conquer
this quaking intimidation drilled into
me as child, this fear of men behind
desks or wearing stethoscopes or
standing before a chalk board, I might
have some prayer of equal footing
when you deign to speak to me again.
I need a suit of armor and a lance,
not these soft clothes that cling to
me like seaweed, this stricken, pale
face that hovers over my shoulders
like a ghost. I look vanquished
before you begin the charge,
cringing by the castle gate in the
guise of a coward. But I am braver
than you think. I have battled
fiercer foes than you, with scars
to prove it. I can stand my ground
when you scowl and bluster, throw
your intellect down like a gauntlet.
What I can't bear is this ominous
quiet, this space before the sentence
begins. I imagined soldiers going mad
under fire, but it's waiting for the
first shot that does them in.

Blackberry Picking

My mother, reaching into the underbrush with
her square hand the color of wheat ripening,
pulled a blackberry from its
leafy mooring and popped it into her
mouth. The silver
pail she carried was filled with dusky fruit that

bubbled at the seams like clumps of caviar on
a spoon. She looked wild as
the brambles with her thorn-pricked fingers
and bare legs streaked with dirt. I would remember
her this way in the cool of the evening,
her torn flesh covered by oven mitts,
placing a steaming
cobbler on the dinner table.
I would feel a strange clutch in my heart,
the impossible-to-describe ache of love that

can never be fully expressed or explained,
shimmering between us like mist
rising from a field of summer berries.

The Call

There is too much noise; the
whirring of a ceiling fan, the blare of television,
the patter of rain against the roof,
a flow of conversation that I cannot follow.

I want only to sink into myself
to a place where the beating of my heart
is like a distant train rolling in its tracks.
Here, without distraction, the rhythm of your breathing

comes to me again, like the pounding of the ocean
to some small creature born in the sand. The pull
is irresistible, though the journey ahead is
fraught with peril. I have abandoned

my safe burrow, quivering with the
unfamiliar sensation
of movement, blinded by the light of the sun,
hungry for something I can only imagine.

I come to you like this, because there is nothing
else. The lure of you, beckoning, has
called me into the fray, and I will follow this
sound if it takes eternity to reach it.

Supplication

On the steps of the cathedral, a man
tossed buckets of water so the
beggars could not kneel. The woman,
draped in black veils,
was undaunted.

She moved from the steps to the
ground, lay full length on her belly,
and lifted her palm like the head
of a swan, rising from
deep water.

Concerto

One's heart breaks to the music of violins,
the plaintive glide of a bow over strings.

It is the sound of loss, of longing so deep that
its graceful frame cannot contain it.

Notes spill over the wood and dance
like ballerinas turning and turning

until they are spent. Images of love's last
lingering glance, a soul rent in

half by parting, disappear like petals
floating on a stream. Nothing remains

but the memory of softness, the haunting
echo of lovers whispering in the dark.

Birdsong

There was a sparrow
on my porch rail
this morning whose song
vibrated her throat
and shook

her feathers in all
their muted
shades of brown and gray,
as if the energy expended by

this frail body propelled
the earth on its daily spin. She
sang for seconds only, opening
her beak wide enough

to swallow the
sky. Then she flew away, as if
she had done at last, the thing she
had been made for.

In Memoriam

One afternoon, he lost his cane. He had to find it
because he was no longer aware of one
side of his body. He quipped that the cancer
would "go to his head" eventually, but I
was unprepared. His mind was his
best feature next to his eyes, which
crinkled kindly when he smiled, and shone
with fierce intelligence.

He was distraught at his forgetfulness, lurching
through the house in desperate search,
lopsided and awkward as a lobster with
one claw. He knocked pictures
askew in the hallway, muttered curses
under his breath, damning himself
for a useless cripple and finally
a coward, once he found the

cane where he left it, hanging on a nail
in the garage. He was afraid, he said, not afraid to
die, but that he wouldn't die well. He didn't want
to disgrace his family, his friends, or himself.
"I can't do this!" he said, his face ravaged
and stricken with panic. (But of course he did
do it, with humor and unflinching courage). In
that moment; however, he was facing

the executioner alone while I was glowing with
health, the sand falling through my hourglass in slow
motion. How terrible it must feel, to be trapped in a
mine shaft when a few feet over your head,
people are going about their
daily lives, thinking of golf
games and homework and how to
unclog the drain. It seems that

disaster is simply a matter of location.
If only we could turn back the clock—go right
instead of left, flip the switch on the coffee pot,
take the long way home, eat more vegetables,
or best of all, have no concept of
mortality. If this was our trade for Eden,
let's give back the stupid apple and
keep our friends.

Just Watch Me

I can be Parisian, you'll see, smoke Gitanes
in long black holders,
blow rings in the air, stain your collar with dark lipstick.

I can be sophisticated, observe you from a distance,
care less with whom you are entwined

as long as you pencil me in the schedule. I can laugh louder, a
sound brittle as glass breaking on stone. I can make love to
other men like coughing into my hand, and think as little of it.
I can wear slim dresses

and stiletto heels that click on the street

like ice picks—sleep naked under a cool sheet, dreaming
of nothing at all. Just watch me, you with your
heavy-lidded eyes and golden skin,
watch me pretend
I don't love you until you
touch me, uncovering the lie like a bone.

Office Slave

Every day she blow-dries her hair and back-combs
her bangs until they look like a claw on her forehead,
pulls on a pair of control-top pantyhose and
squeezes into a skin-tight skirt and whatever blouse she
can lay her hand on in the jumbled closet. She drinks two
cups of coffee and reads the comics. She brushes her teeth
and puts on "Cabernet" lipstick because it brightens
her smile, although she seldom smiles. She steps
into sensible shoes instead of the slinky sandals
that make her feet ache. She pours dry food
into a bowl for the cat, checks the coffee pot to make
sure she turned it off so the house won't burn down.
She grabs her purse and keys and drives the long
way to the office because the interstate is full of lunatics
with road rage. She pulls into the parking deck, takes
the short walk to her building, and waits for the elevator with
the rest of the morning herd. When she reaches her floor,
she flips on the lights because she's the first to arrive
and the last to leave every day. She opens her office door
to discover the cleaning crew had pizza for dinner;
the smell of onions and pepperoni will linger for hours.
She locks her purse in the drawer because someone stole
ten dollars the last time she forgot and left it open.
She turns on the computer and begins making her way
through the piles of paper on her desk as the
clock on the wall ticks off her life in sixty
second increments. For lunch, she brought a salad,
but there's a candy bar in the filing cabinet that she
won't be able to resist later. Her office has no
windows so she has no clue what might be happening
outside—sun, wind, rain, hail, a motorcade of public
officials, maybe the president driving by. The afternoon
drags along until at last, it is 5:30 p.m., the time she
usually looks up from her computer screen to check
the clock. She packs her things and turns out the
lights—the sun, wind, rain, or hail assailing her

her as she exits the building, depending on the time of
year. She drives home on autopilot, pulls her compact
car into the driveway and struggles to open the stubborn
lock on her front door. She grabs a frozen dinner from the
freezer, tosses it in the microwave and changes into a gown
and robe while it heats. She eats at a folding table in front
of the television set, feeding the cat spare scraps from
her plate while the evening news blares the day's catastrophes.
She throws away the cardboard container and puts her fork
and glass in the dishwasher when she is done. She calls
her mother, washes a load of laundry, polishes her toenails,
takes off her makeup, and turns down the covers on her
twin bed at 9:00 p.m. In her sleep, she dreams she is Cleopatra
floating down the Nile on a golden barge, but in the morning
she looks in the mirror and there's her pug nose and double
chin staring back at her like usual, so she does what she always
does when she always does it, and wonders yet again
if monotony could possibly be a fatal condition.

Alpha to Omega

I remember when your words floated like
rose petals in bath water,
tucked under my arm like teddy bears,
piled at the foot of my bed
like sleeping puppies,
caressed my throat like
a silk scarf,
clutched my floured apron like
hungry children,
shimmied around the table like
belly dancers. Now
there are no words, only the sound
of wheels spinning in muck,
the festering of skin around a splinter,
the tap, tap, tap of knife edges on cutting

boards, the persistent scratch of tree
limbs against corneas,

and a feeling cold as creek
water seeping into my shoes.

Ritual

A woman kneels beside a rectangular bronze marker,
the one that says, "Beloved Son." She tenderly cleans it
with her hand, as though he'd

forgotten a spot on his cheek when washing up for dinner.
She reaches into a shopping bag, pulling out a bouquet of
plastic flowers, knowing

anything alive dies too soon. She arranges them neatly in a
vase, as if putting away his toys. She stands, reluctant
to leave, like his first day of

school when she had to drive home without him. She
walks away slowly, as if this time he'll change
his mind and follow.

Traveling Light

The old man on the train from Paris
to Strasbourg polished round glasses
on a faded handkerchief. His only
luggage was a violin case and a
bag of oranges. The girl on the opposite
seat was with her lover, the air between them
electric as winter carpets. A middle-aged
woman had three suitcases, each bigger
than the one before. The young man
rose from his seat and helped her

down the aisle, lifting them
into storage bins. He sat down,
flushed with effort, and asked, "How
do you go about Europe alone with such
heavy bags?" and the woman replied,
her accent thick with paprika and
borsht, "Like this," she said, gazing at him
pointedly. The old man reached for an
orange, and the girl's plump mouth
lifted at the corners, mysterious as the Mona Lisa.

Surrender

Oh, to relive
that moment,
the few seconds
between my body
opening up and
your sweet response,
when there was nothing
for me to do but love
you, only that…a
letting go rather
than a grasping effort,
a letting go and a
soothing peace,
when this and this
and this…the points
where your skin
touched mine
were my entire
universe.

Happiness

Happiness is something sidled
up to, like a child in an orphanage,
moving closer
and closer to an unsuspecting

adult, just near enough to feel the warmth,
to fire the imagination into
believing this is what it must be like
to belong; or the old man

in the park, gazing
at a family having a picnic, closing
his eyes to reveal a vision of
invitation, acceptance, a place in the fold.

He might wander over
after they are gone, place his
hand on the table, hoping to absorb
some remnant of their laughter

into his hollow heart. It is a dog
following a boy, wondering if he could
be the one, the very one
who might reach down and stroke

his fur, take him home, offer him
shelter. It is the woman on the
edge of a party, nursing her
glass, conversation flowing around

her like the hum outside
a fish bowl. She wanders along the
periphery of this group and that, hoping
someone might call her name,

reach out, pull her in. Happiness is
something sidled up to;
a rope that might stop twirling
before your turn to jump.

Vignette

Against a stone wall by the Seine, a man leaned insouciantly,
a cigarette dangling from his mouth. A woman slammed
her fist into his chest and turned away, facing the river.
Behind her back, the man grinned, flicking his ashes
with practiced nonchalance. She was a nondescript
creature, without the usual flair for presentation so
admired in her culture. Her hair was the drab blond
of peeling stairwells and water left too long in the
sink. Her body was adolescent, though lines radiated
from her eyes which made another argument. The man
was beautiful, to put it simply, and was probably never
alone long enough to brush his teeth.

He took another drag and dropped the cigarette
to the ground. He touched the woman on the shoulder,
and she turned to him. As she moved, a bra strap fell
down across her arm. It was a rich, deep red, the color
of Valentines and fire trucks, and explained everything.

When he kissed her, she didn't protest, while smoke
from the cigarette kept rising like a genie from a bottle.

Strawberries

I stood, slicing strawberries, the sun pouring
through the open window and the
crisp autumn day unfolding like party
napkins, with all their riotous color.

The knife shook in my hand
so I set it down gently, and waited for
the tremor to pass. Instead it spread, like a
virus, until my legs failed me.

I thought I could borrow you now and
then, like a cup of sugar, that there would
be no reckoning. I tried to see it your
way, to seize the moment, but the

moments came and went, like house
guests at a floating shower. If I could scratch
your name in my skin, to leave some mark
of your passing, it might convince me

you were here. Your name, however,
remains a secret, since you were never mine.
I can only whisper it when I am alone,
knowing this incantation will not

summon you. There is no magic spell to free
us; no charm can change the past.
There is only now, a woman weeping on
the floor, a bowl half-filled with strawberries.

Dulce Melos
(The Hammered Dulcimer)

Beneath a hammer
the sweetest melody
is shaped,

the most transcendent
rapture released
from its

chamber. Left standing
in the corner,
it collects

dust. Laid across the
knees of angels,
the strings

tremble on bridges
like lovers
parting.

Odalisque

Why you married me I don't know—
because you need a peasant wife,
the thick-knuckled, ruddy-skinned, birth-the-baby-in-the-field
kind of woman who bakes bread and folds towels
the proper way.

She would never leave dirty dishes stacked
like a New York skyline in the sink
or bits of cabbage in the drain.
There would be no ring-around-the-tub
or canned spinach on the table.

She would grow her own vegetables and
serve them in an ochre bowl
beside the fricasseed chicken and
a jar of pickled beets.
But you chose me,

a woman with soft, translucent skin, indolent
shoulders that recline against feather
pillows like sleeping cats,
and a kohl-rimmed gaze that scarcely skims
the cluttered floor.

Eating Watermelon in Granddaddy's Back Yard

Uncut, it sits directly
in the center of
a table spread with newspapers, beside

a sharp knife and plastic salt shaker.
It is round and striped green

as a monochromatic beach ball, but a
good thump yields
the promise of treasure

inside, like a pirate's chest filled with
rubies. We wait impatiently as
Granddaddy, (the sleeves of his crisp cotton
shirt rolled to the elbow),

slices it down the
middle and makes the pronouncement,
"Now THIS is a perfect watermelon,"

which he always does, being
an expert at finding the best melon
on the truck.

The halves separate like
the Red Sea parting for Moses and the
divvying
up begins. Our mouths water in eager
anticipation of the juicy

pulp on our tongues, the quenching
of thirst and sating
of hunger, all in
the same
bite. At last we have it,

a sweet canoe of fruit
that we eat while standing up, spitting seeds
in the grass as

yellow jackets buzz
by our heads and
hover over the table, excited by
the rinds resting
in emerald splendor, bowed like
toothless grins.

Discarded Things

I have developed compassion for discarded things,
foil wrappers, rusty cans, greeting cards, broken furniture,
chipped glasses, milk cartons, pop tops, twisted nails,
chewing gum, outdated magazines, syringes, matches, plastic bags,

newspapers, old women. They've been flung to the sidewalk,
dumped in the trash, left beside the curb, thrown from
speeding cars, crushed under heels, ignored, forgotten, lost.
(I have felt the whoosh of air through which my body

fell, the heat of pavement, the clatter of my bones against the ground).
Do they remember what it's like to be of use, to be significant—
to encompass, to contain, to cheer, to support, to be filled, to nourish,
to open, to hold together, to be tasted, to be understood, to protect, to

burn, to shelter, to inform, to love? Can a bowl that once held
apples with their tart flavors and promises of pie, reconcile itself
to the lonely darkness, the musty solitude of the attic? Or the tin
can smashed under the wheels of a truck adjust to a flat

existence, or a candy wrapper give up its sugary scent for the
smell of garbage? To exist with no purpose is a kind of hell,
and surely it's prima facie that the atoms and molecules of the
animate and inanimate know the pang of becoming unnecessary.

Torre Guelfa

From the tower of the Torre Guelfa,
two ladies, no longer young, sip the Piazza
della Signoria and the Via Tornabuoni, with their
Tuscan wine. In identical voices, they claim

boredom with *Firenze*, the red roofed
villas with flowers spilling from the
windows, motorcycles roaring
through narrow streets, the laugh of a

gypsy child rosy-cheeked and innocent
as a Botticelli angel, his hand wrapped around a
wallet while his mother folds money
in her scarf. The world bellows

below them in all its rage and tumble,
its moaning and writhing, its
arch and cry. They are two thin
birds perched on the edge

of a railing, shifting their feet
while a man scoops water
from a white bowl to cleanse
his face for a kiss.

Snake

It isn't fair
that you can slither
close to people
with your forked
tongue and
soft hiss, like an
indrawn breath
before biting
an apple.
Every snake
should have
a rattle,
a warning sound
that gives a
fighting
chance to
avoid the slow
poison of its
bite. Instead
you strike
without
admonition,
sliding
into the bushes,
while the
wounded
die
alone.

Man in the Metro Station

Lost in the metro and wouldn't you know it
a man is hitting the wall with an empty cardboard

cylinder that might have held a poster
or salad tongs or photographs of

prima ballerinas. He is the color of mountains
stark with winter, the earthen cradle of

sleeping trees. His eyes are wild and of course
nothing he mumbles makes sense because I

don't speak French. Perhaps he is arguing
with concise, Aristotelian logic and the wall

tiles will not concede the point.
In any case, where the hell am I and

how do I get to the Bois de Vincennes
I say aloud, staring at the unintelligible map while

the man walks towards me raising the
cylinder, closer and closer until he is

near enough to point the way.

Cutting Loose

With trepidation and heightened
awareness, your body starts
to move even as your
mind sends signals that people
are watching
and judging. You begin to think that
you will not, after all, lose
yourself in this
music. Every muscle stiffens
and dancing becomes another
rote action like
taking an elevator to the office.
Then suddenly and without

warning a note resonates beyond its
sound into a vibration like
a tuning fork resting
against your spirit. The

body begins to loosen, responding
to this shift in focus with joyous

abandon. You are no longer listening
to the song; you are the song,
resembling a creature
both divine
and earthbound, swiveling your
hips like the frantic swing
of church bells in gale force winds.

Jack of Hearts

I can't be staying long, she said,
her eyes rolling around the room like
bells in a cat toy. He watched her silently, his hands
heavy on his knees, veins throbbing
and running like jumper cables down his muscular arms.

Suit yourself he said in a tight voice, wondering
why she vexed him so, if she showed
up just to taunt him with her unavailability.

It was like she knew exactly when he
was coming up for air, when moving on
was the order of the day instead of going

under. His heart was thumping
like a dog's tail on a hardwood floor, and something
weighty settled on his chest. She was

too beautiful, this woman with her yellow
hair and easy smile, but he wasn't fooled
by it anymore. He knew her skin, soft
and tender as a baby bird, was
fresh bait on a rusty hook,
and the taste still lingered like

metal in his mouth.
I need a little cash, she said, you know,
to tide me over until pay day.
I have a job, not much of a job, but it

pays the bills mostly. Anyway, I was
sick last week and my check was short. I
was wondering if you might loan me
enough to help pay the rent. She

stood there, chewing her lip,
probably wondering how
much influence she still had, if
her light touch on his wallet would glean

the result she was looking for. He let her
suffer a while, because he never
claimed to be a saint. He could hear the
clock in the back room ticking beside
the bed where he slept alone, and the
drip of the kitchen faucet, faint
as a pulse. He was almost ashamed of
himself when he reached in his back pocket,
the naked look of salvation in the
final hour that marked her features.

So, it was like that. She was back on drugs. Nothing
else would make her come to him, of course. He
should have known, could tell now by the way

her muscles twitched under the skin like
rats in a sack. He gave her three hundred
dollars, which he'd never see again, and maybe
not her either this time. She grinned like he was
a man and not an easy mark, and was gone
before he could summon the courage to
watch her leave. He sat for an hour

without moving, the wind lifting
the curtain on the living room window like the hand

of a ghost. When his stomach starting growling,
he got up to make dinner. A soul can burn
forever, but a body has to eat.

Hsi Ling Shi

A woman, juxtaposed with
damp, gray buildings on the edge of
Chinatown,

raised her arm to hail a taxi.
She wore a lavender cheongsam,
her hair dark

as a lacquered tea bowl
against the silky fabric. She
could have

graced the palace of an emperor,
been the inspiration of a thousand
perfect poems.

She deserved a palanquin with
four bearers and a cushion for her
feet, not the

shabby car that carried her away, like a
sprig of lilacs dropped into a
muddy stream.

Fair Divided Excellence

Your touch, light as
powdered sugar on the swell
of my breasts, will linger with
me through the hours

of this parting. Roses opening
slowly, the skim of pink
over the mountains,
the blush of wine against a

crystal goblet—
all remind me of my body and
its blood rising to meet you.
I reach for you in

dreams where your
presence is solid as landfall,
where I lie beside
you like a garnet, glowing,

to awaken with empty
hands like a clumsy thief.

Fourth of July in Lewisville Square

The crowd waits for the perfect palette, when
darkness blackens the sky like the cover on a bird cage. Faces turn
upward as patriotic music blasts the air

and fog rises from the swarthy ground like the ghosts of fallen soldiers.
Children halt in their frenzied tracks, pointing

their mustard-tinted fingers when the first boom sounds and a ball of fire

hurls toward heaven. There is a burst of brilliant sparks that cascade
in trails like the arcing branches of weeping willows.
A collective "ahhh," as if a thousand
people lowered themselves into a hot bath all at once

punctuates each explosion until the finale, when everyone claps and cheers
the cinematic display of color and cacophony. The world becomes

a garden of light, row after row of night blooming flowers that fade

and die in an instant. Finally the last streak of flame fizzles out and billows
of smoke float above the square like

zeppelins. People begin to stir as if waking from a dream,
gathering lawn chairs, blankets and coolers, beginning the long trek to
their cars, dragging dogs on leashes and tired
children by the hand, mosquito

bites swelling on their bodies like dough. Next year, they think,
we'll find a better place to park.

The Comforter

Oh, child, don't
take it so
to heart; do you

imagine he thinks
of you?
You were

a hallway in an
empty
house. He heard

the echo of his
footsteps
there, never a word

you said,
not one. You might
have been

whispering your
dreams
to that copper kettle

on the stove.
Men like him
aren't worth the

price of their
boot laces.
You can't let

it break you, girl.
You are stronger
than that.

Moon Flowers

There is a shy night-blooming
plant kissed by moths and
bats, gleaming in my garden

in phosphorescent clusters.
Its dainty leaves creep through the
trellis, falling like tendrils of hair

against an alabaster cheek.
Its sweet scent is powerful for
such fragile blossoms, as though

a young girl has doused herself
in a harlot's perfume. When
morning comes, all trace

of its beauty and fragrance has
vanished, as if the sun is a
bridegroom abandoned at the altar.

A Clash of Vikings

Against the mustard backdrop of a wall in the Ristorante
Paganini, he leaned back in his chair, an unlit cigarette cradled
against the soft pad of his palm. Elegantly dressed, he
was perhaps a business man in Stockholm, treating himself to

lunch in Gamla Stan. He was much too comfortable to be a
tourist, his eyes hooded and slightly remote from the scene
like a husband who has seen the same woman naked too many
times. His arm stretched across the yellow tablecloth was

still as a snake in a pool of brackish water. Even when
a man, perhaps ten years older, sat down at his table,
he did not move. It was his expression, which froze
like water in a silver ice tray, and the subtle twitch of a nerve

along his cheek that betrayed his awareness of an enemy
breaching the boundary line. He said nothing as his
unwelcome companion spoke at length while gesturing wildly,
his coat bunching across thick shoulders like plates shifting

over the mantle of the earth. When he stood, the interloper
seemed to make one last plea, grabbing his arm so abruptly
that the cigarette fell from his hand. It rolled across the floor
and his eyes grew hard as the homogenous steel of a Viking

blade. The man released him at once, as if stunned by a
blow. One had the sense, after he left the room and merged
with the crowds strolling down Västerlanggatan, that his
gaping foe had been quietly and thoroughly vanquished.

Sweet Dreams

Perhaps he was a reflection
in a pool of water,

or some dream she had in a fitful
sleep. A man's hand

slid down her spine
like the frets of a *kithara*.

She turned to him, reaching—
S'agapo, he whispered,

his voice soft as summer
rain, his fingers splayed

like orange
slices on her belly.

Meeting Rita Dove

I stood in line clutching her book,
a middle-aged white "girl" dressed
like Jackie O. There she was: a legend,
an African-American Queen
with more presence than a room full
of presidents. She gleamed and beamed
at the trail of admirers, especially the
young ones, those who might yet
be something, those for whom the role
of "somebody" hasn't slipped through
their fingers like a dish.

(Pearls are small consolation for the
loss of possibility).

I wonder if heaven is like this,
a woman waiting for God's
signature on a gate pass, the one
that says beloved, treasure, mine,
longing for the slightest indication that
she is not, after all, invisible.

Family Reunion at Lake Mälaren

Light reflected from the lake and filtered
through lilac branches falls across the
open songbook, its pages worn and

yellowed with age. He sings without
glancing at the words, as if holding them
in his calloused hands is enough.
His eyes, in fact, are focused beyond
the artfully adorned room with its
crystal vase of wildflowers and tatted

lace doilies lying like snowflakes frozen
to the backs of chairs, or even the rapt
audience of family and friends, whose
smiling faces reflect their affection
and warm regard. He is traveling

where the music takes him, to a
moment captured in a corridor of
memory, set free for the length of a song.

Grief

It is abnormal, this grief that never ends. I have
become too fragile, as if one step might
shatter my body
into a thousand pieces. I hold
myself lightly in my own
palms, wondering how this hot heart
survives in such a
delicate container. I feel everything—the points of a star,
the rise and fall of a sparrow's breast on

a distant branch, the heat in a halo of light
on the countertop. I walk
in circles, going nowhere. I enter rooms
without remembering why I came. Food has no
enticement, nor drink, nor sleep.
Each night is black, like a chalk board
against which my dreams scratch messages of loss. (I
remember when nights lingered like soft kisses on the brow

of morning). I float through the days,
weightless, revolving,
not attached to anything. My voice is like
an echo in a deep
cave. I call but there is no answer. The movement of air is
like moth wings against my flesh, but it is
only the flutter of my own pulse that touches
me. I crouch in the darkness, pour
earth over my head—mourn without hope of consolation.

Pillow Lava

Deep in a seabed,
lava forms

in the shape
of pillows.

Strange that such
volcanic violence

erupts in so
innocent a shape.

If nothing else, it
reminds us:

be careful where
you lay

your head.

Waiting Up

The most beautiful music might be the sound of a violin
wafting over a balcony, where two lovers dine under a
full moon; or upon awakening on a spring morning, hearing

the bright chatter of birds as they feather their nests; or
perhaps the cry of a newborn baby, the arrival of whom
is the answer to years of ardent prayer; but my own

perception of a heavenly melody sweeter than angels
singing is the sound of my daughter's car gliding into
the driveway, her footsteps pounding across the porch,

her key turning in the lock at two a.m. on a Friday
night. A mother waiting for her child to come home
after dark sees the world like a Halloween carnival,

filled with leering monsters waiting behind every
curve to devour the one person we cannot live without.

The New Me

Who is this woman in the mirror with her wild
gray hair standing on end,

the nice brunette parts lying limp as
cowards? I've been possessed by a harridan,

a militant combative who takes on cant like
some mythical goddess with a

quiver-full of thunderbolts. I used to be such a people-pleasing
doormat in my misspent youth,

and now I want to please myself, and then possibly you, if I'm in
the mood. I can't bear the slightest

hint of emotional dishonesty. (I'll swoop down like a pterodactyl
and tear it to shreds!) Watch out for us,

the ladies who've reached a "certain age." We can spot a phony
at fifty paces, and we won't be polite.

Tommy

Chubby intrusion, crawling into my world
like a roly-poly, following me like a shadow
after mastering the art of doddering about
on your plump feet. Double rows
of black eyelashes and dimples like half-moons
in your round cheeks were hardly fair
on a boy, and should by rights have been
mine. You grew on me, finally, with your
cheerful persistence, your unceasing

adoration of your big sister, who you once said
was prettier than all the girls at school. I
became accustomed to your sleeping bag
on my floor when you had nightmares, the
clutter of your boyish treasures
scattered among my dolls. I did protest against
that jar of garter snakes, nasty writhing
things like miniature sea serpents which
I begged you to toss in the woods. (The thought

of me being afraid of something caused
you no end of delight). And later, when we
went our separate ways—you with
your friends and me with mine—there remained
a bond between us at times tenuous
and others strong as links in an anchor chain,
like when you stopped your car and
commanded your best buddy to get out
because "no one insults my sister."

I wonder what kind of man you might have been
if you hadn't disappeared with such unbelievable
finality, like a door slamming—and if I would
have lived less fully without the sense of
carrying on for both of us, trying to make it up to
you for missing out. What I am certain of is this:
every loss leads back to mourning you,
as if there was only one real
death, and the rest reverberations.

Resort

Outside the door, the sound of laughter and
the soft syllables of Caribbean French

conjure images of sugar cane and bananas,
lush rain forests and sputtering volcanoes,

beaches with sand like granulated sugar,
air hot and moist as my damp towels,

tossed in the corner. It seems to me that
women who speak two languages, whose

faces are dark and mysterious as wishing
wells, who laugh and sing while cleaning

messes they didn't make, are the real people,
while the guests—transient, hysterical for

faux fun, lathered up with sunscreen like
buttered scones—are nothing but cartoons.

The Furies

Ravening maws of clenched
hate that gobble babies like
canapés, swallowing the deeds
of good and evil indiscriminately.
Churches, brothels,

synagogues, sweatshops, they are
all grist for your gorge. You
care nothing for fathers
on their knees in prayer, mothers
working two jobs to feed their

families, children laughing
in a playground—you eat them all,
using pregnant women for toothpicks.
Will you be satisfied when you have
devoured the earth, spitting its serrated

pieces into black holes until there
is nothing left to despise?

Moonlighting

One night my father went out
after dinner and when I asked
where he was going, my mother said,
"moonlighting."

At four years old, my mind ran
amuck with this image. I pictured him
swinging from

star to star until he reached

the moon and flipped a switch marked,
"beams." When it was time for bed,

I wrapped my skinny little arms around
the closest stuffed animal (there

were enough to fill the ark),
and focused on the moon
framed by the window, searching

for my father's face.
I didn't see him but I hoped he could
see me—that he was

watching over our house

like a guardian angel in case
monsters showed up
in my closet. It

was almost as good,
but not quite, as having
a daddy down the hall.

Night Nurse

Lying in a hospital bed with a desperate
illness is not a haven for rest. There is
no sleeping between the blood pressure
and temperature checks, the I.V. adjustments,
doors slamming, people talking at the
nurses' station, and the intermittent moans
of less than optimally drugged patients,
occasionally including yourself. One hospital
had an electric train, complete with
whistles. It never stopped going around
the track, hour after hour. In my delirium,
I wondered when it would come for me.

Of all the medical personnel, including
the doctors, night nurses inspire
the most dread, or the sweetest comfort.
They rule the floor from dusk to dawn,
and you are at their mercy. Some I've
known would have found careers in
concentration camps. Others are like
angels visiting, their hands smooth and
dry as cornstarch on your skin. So many
defenseless subjects under their
complete control, no family members
to stand guard, no doctors to write

orders until morning, must dredge
their personalities for whatever lies at
bottom. I've known nurses with
layer after layer of kindness, all the
way through. But others, the ones who
make you sweat without fevers, would
strangle you with your own I.V. line if no
one would find you in the morning. In
lieu of that, they practice more subtle tortures.
The button to call them is useless; they come
when they please and hope it is too late.
With them, you're on your own.

Beach House

I remember a house bathed in light. The sun
settled on the roof and flowed down the weathered
boards like dollops of French vanilla ice cream
melting on a waffle cone. It warmed

the panes of sparkling glass and created yellow
designs on the honeyed wood of the knotty
pine walls. There was no darkness in that
house. Even when night came and the

sun dipped into the steely blue Atlantic, there
were lamps in the corners and nightlights
in every bedroom which outlined our pale
limbs under freshly laundered sheets. And outside

the door, fireflies punctured the gloom with their
brilliant bodies and moonlight coated the
yard with faint but luminous rays, like a fine
layer of talcum powder on a faded floor.

Casting the Second Stone

The first stone was the easy one.
Before that point, it was still
an idea. There was no thump of rock
against bone from which to recoil.
There was only accusation,
condemnation, and the frenzy of
a crowd eager for "justice"
to be done.

A stone was rather
harmless sitting in one's
palm, after all. And throwing it, well, how
many were pitched haphazardly
in boredom when every path
contained hundreds? It might have
be been one of them until it hit the
human target.

The next stone; however, tossed after
the cry of pain, the spilling of blood,
changed the dynamic of the
moment. There was no more pretense of
childish games.

The one who cast the second stone knew
exactly what he was doing.

Going Nowhere

He's walking with the sound of waves pounding in his ears
like thunder and the frigid water eddying
around broken shells
and bits of sea glass, reaching for his feet. It's so cold
he can't feel his fingers buttoning

his jacket, and the wind whips
and whistles around him like a herd of displaced demons.
Clouds move in and cover the stars and the moon is
like a cue ball in a side pocket, lost from view. Thoughts flap like
seagulls scavenging

in his head, picking out long-discarded memories of people and
places he used to know. He remembers
turning the corner on his street,
his eyes heavy with sleep, a lamp in the window beckoning
like the exit from a tunnel. A blast of

wintry air salts his lungs, clearing visions
of welcome from the deserted beach. Quickening his pace, he
follows the line of houses looming
beyond the dunes like the serrated spine of a sleeping
dragon, stretching towards a

single point of amber light. He stares until the image
blurs, bobbing with the brisk
motion of his gait like a lit cigar dangling from the mouth
of an auctioneer, to whom he would bid
anything for a destination.

Mid-Summer of My Childhood, 1965

There is a listlessness
in the air, a droop of a hand,
the slope
of a shoulder.
Everything sinks to
the ground as if the
world is fainting. Dusk is a stain
spreading over faded
carpet, and lamps are

bursts of flame.
Sleep soaks our hair
and dampens the
skin behind our knees until
we are slick and swollen
as garden snails. I dream of ice cold
milk in a metal tumbler,
rain blowing
through an open window.

Hummingbirds

Iridescent miracles of flight
with invisible wings

and fragile forms, hummingbirds
spend their days

in search of nectar. In the wake
of gentle zephyrs, they

dart from flower to flower,
burying their slender

bills in fragrant blossoms. Their
breath's ambrosia sweetens

the air as they hover in our gardens,
their mosaic colors majestic in

miniature, like tiny sparks from
Northern Lights.

Kingston Mines (Chicago, 2003)

He was so feeble they helped
him onstage, skin ashy and tough
as elephant hide, a tan suit
and wide-brimmed hat set at a jaunty
angle. Somebody handed him
a guitar and he held it like a woman

on his lap, tender and reverent with an
edge of possession. You could see
what he used to be beneath the
scrim of old age, as soon as he started
to play. His fingers found their
way around that fret like a man revisiting
a street where he grew up, uncertain
at first but picking up speed as he went
along, remembering everything.

If you closed your eyes, you might be in
Mississippi, the sun like a hammer
cracking the ground and heating up young
men's blood until it ran like lava
in their veins, pulling them out of their
houses and cars into every kind

of trouble. You knew he was in
the thick of it, sweat running in
rivulets down his face, his legs strong
and hard as cherry wood. And the hurt of
losing it all was there in every note,
like something moaning in the
underbrush, but joy was there, too—swift,

pure pleasure that rose under
his hands and filled the room until
anybody who wasn't moving to that music
had to be dead. When it was over,
the silence was so profound it could
have been a eulogy for a holy man and
you never know, maybe it was.

Love

Love is the flutter of a veil, falling,
the chill nakedness of an indeterminate fate.
It is the lift of a hand, beckoning,
the untwisting of limbs and the long walk.
It is the swift intake of breath, the
smooth transition from noun to verb. Love

is a thumb that breaks the skin,
the teeth that tear the succulent fruit
from its soft, white rind, the fragrant
peeling left on a bare table.

Play Ball

Beneath the artificial light, our mothers looked like
movie stars with their red lipstick
and shirts tied at the

waist, waving cigarettes in the air like
conducting batons. Our fathers broke their concentration
from time to time, smiling at them like teenage boys
spotting their dates across a high school gym.

They would spit on their hands and wield a bat
until the resounding crack propelled them to first base, their feet
churning red dust that stained their clothes and

rose in clouds as if they were
magicians in a disappearing act. Our mothers
whistled and cheered no matter what their

husbands did, while we caught lightning bugs in
jelly jars and darted under the bleachers.
As dusk folded into dark, children gathered in the
stands, leaning against each other like puppies in a basket

until the game ended and we were packed in
the back seats of assorted family cars. Full of
root beer and hotdogs, sunburned and
played out, we were lulled to sleep

by the murmur of our parent's voices, the night
air rushing over half-rolled windows, and the spin of our perfect
world, heading towards home plate.

Acknowledgements

First and foremost, I am grateful to God for His unconditional love, and for all the blessings and miracles in my life, including a wonderful family and a host of very exceptional friends—too many to name. I must extend special thanks, however, to the following: Nelson Adams, Connie Cline and Anne Blackman, for their invaluable editorial assistance, friendship and constant support; Mark C. Houston, M.D., and Susan Nagel-Bloch, for their friendship, support and continued interest in this project; my parents, Tom and Loretta Kirby, for a lifetime of love and encouragement; my adored uncle, Stephen White, for the stunning piece of art on the cover; the late Robert M. Kerr, M.D., beloved friend and mentor, who advised me to take writing seriously and myself lightly; the late Thomas ("Tommy") M. Kirby, Jr., my "little" brother and faithful childhood companion; my lovely and talented daughter, Gia, for the joy of being her mother; and my husband, Leonard Erickson, for his computer expertise and loving support. Thank you all, from my heart.

About the Author

Terri Kirby Erickson is the mother of a grown daughter, Gia Riana, and a freelance editor and writer, visual artist and poet. She lives with her husband, Leonard, next-door to two of her very favorite children, Madison and Max, in a small town in North Carolina. *Thread Count* is her first book of poetry.

Printed in the United States
47964LVS00003B/280